ESFP:
Understand And Break Free From Your Own Limitations

MATTHEW BRIGHTHOUSE

Copyright © 2018

Table of Contents

TABLE OF CONTENTS 2

INTRODUCTION..3

1 THE FINE LINE BETWEEN STRENGTH & WEAKNESS 6

2 LEARN TO NOT TAKE EVERYTHING PERSONALLY...................15

3 LEARN TO FACE CONFLICT HEAD ON 19

4 LEARN TO FOCUS ON THE TASK AT HAND 23

5 LEARN TO PLAN FOR THE FUTURE..26

6 LEARN TO AVOID RISKY BEHAVIOR & SELF-INDULGENCE 29

7 LEARN TO GIVE YOURSELF FULLY TO YOUR PARTNER 32

8 CONCLUSION 35

Introduction

Learning about your personality and what makes you tick is about so much more than entertainment and enlightenment, it's about learning how you tick, how you can change, what you can learn from, and breaking down barriers you might have been putting in the way of your future success. Learning about yourself enables you to get to know yourself much better, gives you information on parts of your make up that you might never have considered, and allows you to delve deeper into your inner psyche.

You've taken the first step towards self-discovery and enlightenment by taking the Myers-Briggs personality test, and by doing that you have identified yourself as an ESFP personality type. Life is certainly not dull when you're around! An ESFP is a born entertainer, someone who loves to be in the spotlight, loves to entertain, loves to make people laugh, and someone who is always reinventing themselves. By taking the test, you showed an interested in wanting to learn about yourself in more detail, so you should pat yourself on the back for that! By doing this, you're showing a willingness to improve, and to push towards success in all areas of your life.

Of course, every personality type has its upsides and downsides, but it's vital to learn about both so you can tweak any changes necessary, and really work towards being the very best version of yourself that you can be. The aim is not to change who you are at your very core, it's about changing the negative things about yourself, usually your weaknesses, that are standing in the way of you reaching your potential; it is about knocking down walls and limitations. You might not even be aware you're putting a big brick wall in the way of your future progression, but by reading this book and learning about your personality traits, and your strengths and weaknesses, you can recognize where work needs to be done. You may be surprised, you may be a little shocked at first, but by delving deep and being totally honest with yourself, you can complete this journey to the best of your ability.

It's vital to point out at this point in time that no part of this book is meant as criticism, that is a point you need to hold firmly in your mind. Everything is meant to be constructive, because in order to learn and grow, sometimes we need to be painfully honest with ourselves. Of course, your personality type has a huge range of fantastic strengths and positive points, and it's vital to celebrate those, whilst also adapting and changing your weaknesses accordingly. Many people love to have an ESFP around, because life is rarely boring, and they often inspire others to go for it and forget the 'what if' in life.

Learning about personality types is a really interesting subject, because not only does it help you and your own self-discovery route, but it also helps you understand other people much better too. Whether you're a people person or not (and the chances are that you are a people person as a hugely sociable ESFP), knowing why a person reacts a certain way is a huge benefit in life.

So, with all that being said, and with the knowledge that your weaknesses do not make you a bad person, it's time to delve a little deeper into the wonderful and entertaining world of the ESFP personality type. It's time to go on a hugely enlightening journey towards self-discovery.

Are you ready?

1
The Fine Line Between Strength & Weakness

You are a human being and that means that you are flawed. It's no biggie, because we are all flawed in some way, and that is what makes us who we are. Can you imagine if everyone was perfect? How boring a world would that be? The key is not to aim towards perfection, but to aim towards being the best version of yourself possible. If you can achieve that, you've broken down every wall you could ever put in your own way, and the rewards will be opportunities that regularly come your way. Imagine if each day you woke up, your goal was to just be a little bit better than yesterday. How much progress would you have made in 6 months? A year?

By taking the Myers-Briggs personality type and identifying yourself as an ESFP type, you are in good company. Such celebrities as Marilyn Monroe, Adele, Jamie Foxx, and Jamie Oliver are all ESFPs, and they all display the traits classically. At this point, however, it's possible that those four letters don't mean much to you at all. With that in mind, let's explore what ESFP stands for.

E – Extrovert
S – Sensing
F – Feeling
P – Perception

Extrovert

You don't need to be a rocket scientist to figure out that an ESFP is someone who loves the spotlight! You're known as the 'Entertainer', which means you enjoy putting on a show, making people laugh, cry (in a good way), and basically giving people a damn good time. Having said that, you aren't an extrovert in a facetious way, you're actually very sensitive and giving with your time and energy. You don't ever make the whole thing about you, and instead, you prefer to focus on the entertainment value, the reaction of the person or people in front of you.

The danger in being an extrovert in any guise is that you can become easily distracted because you're too busy having a good time and entertaining everyone around you. We will talk in more detail later on in the book about how you can learn to focus on the task at hand, how you can learn that boring, routine things in life have to be completed as well as the fun things, and how to incorporate all of that into your life, without suffering in terms of enjoyment. It can be done!

Sensing
You are very sensitive and giving of your time, and you can easily dedicate your entire time to someone who needs your attention. This means that you are a sensing type of person, someone who lives in the here and now and doesn't really give much thought to the future at that point in time. Whilst that is great in many ways because you're really living, there are points in life where you need to think about the future, in order to plan and achieve further down the line. Later on, in the book, we are going to talk about

how you can learn to incorporate planning into your life.

Feeling
We've mentioned that you are an emotional person, and that means that you make decisions based on your gut and your emotions. Being in tune with your emotions is a great thing because it means that you can be guided by your intuition and you can understand the feelings of other people, but at the same time, you need to learn not to let your emotions dictate and rule your life. On occasion, an ESFP can become so emotionally stuck in their own heads that they can't see the woods for the trees. Again, we're going to cover this a little later in the book, so you can learn not to take everything so personally, and how to balance your emotions successfully.

Perception
As an ESFP, you're a very perceptive person, and this is down to your emotions. We have just talked about how you are sensitive, but you're also sensitive to the feelings of others and you can easily pick up on whether there is something wrong with those around you. You can use your perception skills to make decisions and choose the right path in life, provided you can learn to plan a little, and provided you can harness your emotions when they become a little stormy.

Now we know that ESFP actually stands for, we need to delve a little deeper and explore the strengths and weaknesses of your particular personality type.

ESFP Strengths

Because it's always good to be positive first, let's explore your strengths.

Boldness
An ESFP is not scared of taking risks and going outside of their own comfort zone. It's likely that you've taken a travel adventure on your own at least once, and that you probably enjoyed it too, making new friends along the way. You don't struggle to meet people and make connections, it's something you do on a regular basis, and it's a very natural process for you too. Within your social circle, there are likely to be a huge range of different people, who you see from time to time. In addition, you're someone who doesn't hold back, and if you want something, and you feel passionate about it, you'll go out and get it. This is something which is likely to inspire those around you. The key here is to identify the things that you feel that amount of passion for, measure risk versus benefit, before jumping in with both feet.

Originality
There is only one of you! You're likely to be constantly changing your appearance, perhaps dying your hair or changing your style on a regular basis, because you love to express yourself through how you look and come over to other people. Perhaps this is why so many expressive and creative celebrities are ESFP types, such as Adele and Marilyn Monroe. This also extends to the work you do and the way you interact with others too. You are likely to go about things in a totally different way to anyone else, and whilst a lot of the time it works, sometimes it doesn't.

When this happens, you simply shrug your shoulders and try a different route!

Creative
You're artistic, you're someone who loves to put on a show and be different from everyone else. Look at celebrities such as Jamie Oliver, who is also an ESFP. Jamie Oliver is a celebrity chef who has done everything totally different to everyone else and gone about it all in a hugely creative way. Similarly, Adele is another celebrity with this common trait. A few years ago, Jamie Oliver put together a campaign to change the school lunches for children around the UK. He campaigned for healthier and more delicious meals, and he put his heart and soul into it. He did this because he felt passionate about the cause and because he identified a creative twist that he could use. This is a classic trait of an ESFP.

You're a Do-er
You're practical, you're someone who will get the job done and won't sit around wondering 'what if'. If you want to do something, you'll find a way to make it work. You can't handle the thought of not trying because the 'what if' is not something that will ever sit comfortably with you. This is great, provided the thing you're considering is actually practical and not risky. We will talk in greater detail a little later on the ESFPs tendency towards risky behaviors, but from a strengths point of view, you're someone who will certainly do what they say they're going to do, provided you are enjoying the task and provided you identify with it in a passionate way.

ESFP Strengths

Because it's always good to be positive first, let's explore your strengths.

Boldness
An ESFP is not scared of taking risks and going outside of their own comfort zone. It's likely that you've taken a travel adventure on your own at least once, and that you probably enjoyed it too, making new friends along the way. You don't struggle to meet people and make connections, it's something you do on a regular basis, and it's a very natural process for you too. Within your social circle, there are likely to be a huge range of different people, who you see from time to time. In addition, you're someone who doesn't hold back, and if you want something, and you feel passionate about it, you'll go out and get it. This is something which is likely to inspire those around you. The key here is to identify the things that you feel that amount of passion for, measure risk versus benefit, before jumping in with both feet.

Originality
There is only one of you! You're likely to be constantly changing your appearance, perhaps dying your hair or changing your style on a regular basis, because you love to express yourself through how you look and come over to other people. Perhaps this is why so many expressive and creative celebrities are ESFP types, such as Adele and Marilyn Monroe. This also extends to the work you do and the way you interact with others too. You are likely to go about things in a totally different way to anyone else, and whilst a lot of the time it works, sometimes it doesn't.

When this happens, you simply shrug your shoulders and try a different route!

Creative
You're artistic, you're someone who loves to put on a show and be different from everyone else. Look at celebrities such as Jamie Oliver, who is also an ESFP. Jamie Oliver is a celebrity chef who has done everything totally different to everyone else and gone about it all in a hugely creative way. Similarly, Adele is another celebrity with this common trait. A few years ago, Jamie Oliver put together a campaign to change the school lunches for children around the UK. He campaigned for healthier and more delicious meals, and he put his heart and soul into it. He did this because he felt passionate about the cause and because he identified a creative twist that he could use. This is a classic trait of an ESFP.

You're a Do-er
You're practical, you're someone who will get the job done and won't sit around wondering 'what if'. If you want to do something, you'll find a way to make it work. You can't handle the thought of not trying because the 'what if' is not something that will ever sit comfortably with you. This is great, provided the thing you're considering is actually practical and not risky. We will talk in greater detail a little later on the ESFPs tendency towards risky behaviors, but from a strengths point of view, you're someone who will certainly do what they say they're going to do, provided you are enjoying the task and provided you identify with it in a passionate way.

A Sociable, People Person
You have great people skills and your communication skills are top-notch. You're likely to connect easily with others and you speak totally 'as it is'. Many people a drawn to your no-nonsense, yet friendly approach to life, and you're also very sensitive, which means that people feel you are genuine. You're not someone who is likely to confront someone when you feel wronged, and you're not someone who is likely to call someone out on something they've done. Instead, you're likely to go totally out of your way to avoid conflict, which is something we're going to talk about shortly in terms of a weakness. From a strength point of view, however, people don't feel that you're someone who is likely to attack them verbally or criticize them in any way, which means they are more likely to open up to you and show their genuine selves.

ESFP Weaknesses

Now we know what your strengths are, and what fantastic strengths they are, let's discuss your weaknesses and identify where you can start to make some adjustments. Again, because as an ESFP you're quite a sensitive soul, remember not to take any of the following information personally, and instead, see it in the constructive and well-meaning way it is intended.

Very Sensitive
There is nothing wrong with being sensitive, but you are a *very* sensitive person, and it is quite easy to hurt your feelings, often without even realizing it. You tend to put on a mask when you're performing, or out enjoying yourself with a group of people, but

underneath it all, you have a very soft center. At times, you can allow your emotions to get the better of you, and you can't understand much in terms of reality when these emotions take over. It's vital to be able to balance your emotions and keep yourself from becoming down. We will talk in more detail shortly about how you can learn not to take everything so personally and maintain balance. If you can do this, you'll be able to find harmony in many different aspects of life.

Will do Anything to Avoid Confrontation
To say that you're an extrovert, you're actually very scared of confrontation and conflict! Perhaps this is because you are so sensitive and because you're also sensitive to the needs and feelings of others. You don't like to argue and you don't like to be confronted with an issue. The problem is that by trying to avoid these confrontations, you're likely to say whatever you need to say to get out of it. This can cause issues in the future because you might unwittingly end up lying to someone to get out of the situation, and then cause a further conflict! It's a vicious circle, and one we will cover in more detail shortly but for now, recognize this is an area you need to work on to avoid further conflict in the future.

Can Easily Become Bored
You are not someone who enjoys the dull and mediocre things in life, you're always trying to find the next entertaining thing to get your teeth into, and that means that the routine tasks that we all need to do, often go by the wayside. Your tendency to be easily bored can also mean that you can become embroiled in risky behavior, such as spending too

much and getting into debt or airing on the side of self-indulgent. Again, we're going to go over this in more detail shortly, but this can also relate to your romantic relationships in life – you tend to go from person to person because you need someone who can really hold your attention in a special way.

Planning Isn't Your Forte
You're not a planner, and you're not someone who likes to think about what is going to happen in the future. Instead, you live for the moment, and whilst that's great in many ways, it can mean that you never really reach your potential completely because you fail to do the planning required! In life, we all need to think ahead sometimes, perhaps to plan for our financial security, or when it comes to making commitments to a romantic partner. It's not that your commitment adverse, you just don't see the fun in planning. If you can learn how to plan, just a little, or perhaps put some mechanisms into place which allow you to think forwards instead of being stuck in the present day, you'll conquer many of the problems that may currently plague your life.

Can Find it Hard to Focus And Concentrate
The final weakness we're going to talk about is an inability to focus and concentrate for long periods of time. We've mentioned that you get bored easily and in routine tasks, you find it very hard to focus and keep your mind on the game. As we mentioned before, it's important to get the boring stuff out of the way and concentrate to do it all right, before we can get onto the fun stuff. We will cover this later on in the book, to help you find a balance between focusing and fun.

As you can see, an ESFP is an interesting personality type to explore. You have a lot of fantastic and enviable strengths, but you also have a few weaknesses that you can work on. There is room for improvement, and by learning about it, you can work towards reducing the effect your weaknesses may have on your life, knocking down any limitations and walls you're unknowingly putting in your own way. We will now go on to cover the most important and common weaknesses which affect a regular ESFP. Be honest with yourself and identify which ones apply to you. If they do, read carefully, take it all on board, and see where you can make the necessary changes.

2
Learn to Not Take Everything Personally

ESFPs may be extroverted, and they may love to be in the spotlight, but that doesn't mean they are bulletproof in terms of feelings. If you were to be compared to an animal, it would probably be a crab – on the outside you look like nothing is going to faze you, because you're out there, being yourself, being original and doing what you love, but underneath, you have a very soft underbelly, and criticism and words can be very hurtful to you. You probably won't even show when you're hurt, and instead, you'll retreat inside your shell, dealing with the issue alone.

There is nothing wrong with being sensitive because that means you're in touch with yourself and others, but it can become a problem if you allow your emotions to take over and dictate your actions. It's really about balance and finding that balance can be difficult at first. Emotions can be turbulent from time to time, and if you allow yourself to become drowned in what you're feeling, it can be very difficult to find a life jacket and swim, without knocking yourself out on the rocks a few times. You can grab that life jacket though, metaphorically speaking, but it's about developing mental strength and recognizing your own strengths and qualities, not taking everything directly to heart as a criticism.

To further complicate matters, an ESFP is not only sensitive themselves, but they are also very sensitive to the feelings of other people. This is the part of yourself that you shouldn't attempt to tweak in any way because being sensitive to others means that you can connect with them much better, understand them in a way that other people may not be able to, and it means that you can make friends and connections too. The part that you can work on, however, is how easily you allow yourself to become hurt, and how much you allow yourself to feel as a result.

Everyone is criticized in some way, but that doesn't always have to be the wounding thing it may seem. What you can do, is learn to take criticism in a constructive way, and use it to learn and build. You should also stop and think about whether the criticism is actually fair, or whether it is the result of jealousy on someone else's part – totally possible!

At the end of the day, as long as you are doing the best you can, and you're not hurting anyone in the process, criticism should not harm you.

How to Control Your Emotions

Feelings are part of being human, they allow us to experience life in the best possible way. We feel joy, happiness, anger, sadness, and jealousy on a regular basis, and that is what life is about – feeling. What you need to do is understand that not every feeling has to be so extreme, and that you can be angry without it taking over your day and forcing you to act out as a result.

You are not a negative person, so it's not really about learning how to turn negative thoughts into positive ones, but if you allow yourself to become bogged down with a negative emotion, it can be very easy for you to start acting a little like a martyr. This is a common ESFP trait, and something you need to keep an eye out for. So, when someone criticizes you, or you feel low, ask yourself why. Ask yourself if there is any real foundation to the comment or the reason why you feel down. If there is, what can you do about it? Can you change anything?

Putting the control back in your hands will empower you and lift your mood. But, what if there is nothing you can do to change it? In that case, it's likely that you simply need to accept the situation or comment, shrug it off as best you can, and vow to do better next time. Come to terms with the fact that you're human, and that occasionally humans mess up and fail! It's okay, it's part of being alive!

Once you make peace with that fact, you'll find it much easier to avoid falling into that 'woe is me' trap that can occasionally become an ESFP trait. Not everything in life is meant to be personal, sometimes people just vent, and it can seem that they're aiming everything at you, but they're probably not. Have you ever lashed out and perhaps unwittingly thrown shade at someone without even meaning it? Of course you have, you're human! If you have done no wrong, then the comment should just be like water off a duck's back.

Learning to manage your emotions and keep them balanced, rather than allowing them to go off kilter in one direction or the other, will empower you with the strength to really face any situation. Whilst it's not realistic to never expect to be down or low, and for words not to upset you, it's about minimizing the situations and understanding that it is rarely ever as bad as it may seem.

3
Learn to Face Conflict Head on

As an ESFP, you are a master at avoiding conflict. This isn't because you have excellent conflict resolution skills and can calm down a situation easily, it's because you simply run away from them and avoid them at all costs!

You might think that is the best way to never have to face the awkwardness of conflict, but ask yourself this – will the issue simply disappear and never raise its head again? Unlikely! By not facing situations and sometimes having to face conflict as a result, certain issues will always keep coming back into your life and will probably get worse as a result. You could also find that people become frustrated with the whole situation, and with you for running away from it!

If you're not someone who runs away from the conflict, you're likely to be someone who says whatever they need to say to placate the person and get out of the situation. This is not a good option either!

Sometimes in life, we simply need to face the music and deal with whatever comes of it. This is the only way to get to the bottom of a situation and really sort it out so that it never becomes an issue again. If you keep avoiding it, you're just going to put it off until another day, and if you keep saying whatever you need to say to get out of it, and then not doing what you're saying, you're going to frustrate people, and they won't trust your words in the future.

Conflict is part of life, and it isn't direct criticism all of the time. This issue probably ties in with the ESFP tendency towards sensitivity, and you hate the fact that someone is upset with you, angry with you, or has an issue with something you've said or done. You take it personally because you are so sensitive to others, and you're angry at yourself for the situation occurring in the first place. The thing is, by avoiding it, you're just making it worse!

Make a vow to yourself that the next time conflict arises, you will simply face it. It won't be easy the first time, and you'll probably have to fight your instinct to run or blag it out, but keep telling yourself that you're going to make life harder for yourself down the line. You might be all about living for today, but if you're making your coming days harder, they're not going to be much fun either!

Facing a conflict head-on doesn't mean fighting, it doesn't mean arguing, and it doesn't mean getting upset, it means talking calmly about the issue and coming to a suitable piece of middle ground. Conflict resolution isn't a pleasant subject or situation to be in, but if you can learn how to diffuse a situation successfully, then you will find that conflicts and confrontations in the future won't leave you sweating and becoming a flight risk.

So, the next time you're in the face of a conflict or confrontation, remember/do the following:

- Stay calm
- Take deep breaths
- Listen to the other person, and show them that you're listening by nodding, making eye contact, and avoiding negative body language, such as crossing your arms across your body
- Use appropriate language, such as 'I understand', 'I can see your point'
- Take in what the person is saying and think rationally about whether you are at fault or not. You really might not be at fault, but if you are, just admit it; there's no shame in being wrong sometimes
- If you need to apologize, then do so, but if you don't, don't! – We don't always have to say 'sorry' because sometimes we have nothing to be sorry for! If you do have a reason to apologize, however, just do it, the other person will appreciate your honesty
- If the other person is becoming aggressive, either verbally or physically, walk away. Tell them that you're going to walk away until you are both in a calmer place
- Try and come to a resolution - Ask the other person who they would like the situation to be resolved and see if you can agree on a piece of middle ground
- Once the situation is over, reflect and then forget, but make sure you do what you have said you're going to do

It's really that simple, and if you can do all of this, the issue will be solved, forgotten, and nobody will be left feeling resentful or annoyed. After a while, it will become second nature and you will not feel the need to run or squirm your way out of confrontations in the future. Of course, it's best to avoid the need for confrontation or conflict in the first place, but that's not always something we can do!

you make a snap decision. ESFPs are usually highly talented in entertainment circles, and it's not worth damaging or putting at risk a potentially fantastic future, by living too much in the moment and creating a problem that you may not even be aware you're making. Life is about balance, so in terms of cash, if you can afford to make that big purchase you've been dreaming about, only do it if you can afford to pay it back quickly; only go out on that big night out if you don't have commitments the next day; only book that vacation if you can actually realistically afford to go on it, both in terms of money and time.

The best things in life come when we work hard for them and wait, rather than acting spontaneously and going for it when we really don't have the financial capacity or time for it.

7
Learn to Give Yourself Fully to Your Partner

Being in a relationship with an ESFP can be a wonderful thing, but it can be a challenging thing too! You are not someone who likes to be tied down, and whilst you're a great catch, with some fantastic qualities, you're not someone who is likely to look for a long-term commitment actively.

The thing is, an ESFP makes a great long-term partner. You're someone who is very sensitive of the feelings of others, you're sensitive yourself, and you're likely to be an exciting person to be around – one day will rarely be the same as the next. These are great qualities to have as a person, and as a partner, you're probably going to be someone who doesn't struggle to attract a mate.

The problem comes in actually committing to a long-term relationship because you're not someone who likes that tag!

It's not that you're commitment-phobic, because you love to be loved and to give love, but you're not someone who will make plans for the future, as we've mentioned before. This can frustrate a partner who is a bit more forward planning than you are, and give them the impression that you're simply not interested in building a future with them at all. It may not be the case in reality, because perhaps you do want a future with that person, but you're just going with the flow and seeing what happens, what's the rush? Does the other person agree? Probably not. There are many personality types out there who dream of stability and some who even demand it. Some people want the title of a relationship, and they want to know that the union is heading towards something more serious, perhaps marriage and children in the future.

Do you want that? This is something you really need to ask yourself, because if you do, and you continue to be a little 'flakey' and all 'one day' with your partner, they may get tired of waiting and leave to find someone who is a bit more forward with their intentions.

It is likely that as an ESFP you have had several partners, and that isn't meant in a negative way, it is simply that you are likely to become bored and move on, or you fall foul of the situation we just described above. You are not someone who focuses on one person and then commits easily, you are someone who needs encouragement, and perhaps even an ultimatum!

In order to find a partner and stay with them for life, to build the future you want, you need to give your all to that person, and you need to compromise in terms of future planning. If you are serious about them, if you really want to stay with them and don't want the relationship to end, then you need to be honest and open about your feelings. Allow the other person to feel that you're committed, and that you're not just going to up and leave when you become bored or freaked out at the future planning.

How can you do this? You need to picture the worst-case scenario.

If you love someone, how would you feel if they left you? You'd be devastated, right? Now, put yourself in the other person's shoes – you love that person and you want to be with them forever, or as far ahead as you can see anyway. They refuse to show you that they feel that way, although they drop loving hints every now and then. How would you feel? Would you feel frustrated? Would you feel fearful of the future? Would you want to continue living that way? This is why people leave, and it is a very real situation. Picture that situation and allow yourself to imagine how you would actually feel in the event of it happening. Use that raw emotion to make a change, and to compromise with your planning, and perhaps to give your partner that commitment they need. You have to give your all to someone, otherwise, they will feel neglected. Nobody deserves to feel neglected in a relationship.

8
Conclusion

And there we have it, the wonderful, fun, and energetic life of an ESFP. You are one of the world's favorite types of personality because although you're all about the life and soul of the party, you're not all about yourself, and you're not dismissive of the feelings of others.

Of course, you have weaknesses, but before you begin on your journey to self-discovery, by working on your weaknesses and reducing their effect on your life, give yourself a minute to recognize the positives you have in your personality type. You're fun, you're sociable, you're always sensitive to the feelings of other people, you're original, you're creative, and you're bold. They are all fantastic qualities, and you should definitely hold onto those with a firm grip. What you do need to do, however, as with every personality type, is to recognize that along with those strengths, also come weaknesses.

Every single human being on the planet has weaknesses, it's part of being alive. What you can't do however is allow those weaknesses to place blockages and walls in the way of future progression, and what you should do is learn about those points and put into place a plan of action. By reading this book you'll know that ESFPs don't like planning, but if you're going to change everything and make your life a million times more positive and successful, you need to start!

As we mentioned at the start of this book, we're not talking about changing who you are at your very core; as an individual, you are wonderful already, and it's more about making tweaks, in order to push yourself forward and making the biggest success of your life possible. You will also find that by learning about your own personality type, you'll want to know more about the other personality types in the spectrum. This is a great thing to do because it helps you to understand other people and their reactions to situations in life. It's a really interesting subject overall, and if you can use the information you learn to enhance your relationships and interactions with other you'll be on the right track.

It may well be that you don't recognize yourself in every point we have mentioned in this book, and that is because nobody is ever 100% one personality type; we all display traits of the other types to a certain degree. If you find yourself doing this a lot, explore the other types around your ESFP result, and see if there is anything you can learn from the strengths and weaknesses associated with that type too. Identify the points in this book that really call out to you, and work on those first. In order to do that, you need to be truly honest with yourself, even if the truth possibly hurts a little. Nobody is perfect, and nobody should ever strive to be, and there is nothing wrong with having those weaknesses, provided you recognize it and work on self-improvement.

So, we will now bid you goodbye, and leave you with all the advice and information we've given to you. Hopefully, you will use it to put you on your own successful path towards self-discovery and future success in all areas of your life.

Note from the author

Thank you for purchasing and reading this book. If you enjoyed it or found it useful then I'd really appreciate it if you would post a short review on Amazon. I do read all the reviews personally so that I can continually write what people are wanting.

If you'd like to leave a review then please visit the link below:

https://www.amazon.com/dp/B07BNKWNWV

Thanks for your support and good luck!

Check Out My Other Books

Below you'll find some of my other books that are popular on Amazon and Kindle as well. Simply search the titles listed below on Amazon. Alternatively, you can visit my author page on Amazon to see other work written by me.

ENFP: Understand and Break Free From Your Own Limitations

INFP: Understand and Break Free From Your Own Limitations

ENFJ: Understand and Break Free From Your Own Limitations

INFJ: Understand and Break Free From Your Own Limitations

ENFP: INFP: ENFJ: INFJ: Understand and Break Free From Your Own Limitations – The Diplomat Bundle Series

INTP: Understand and Break Free From Your Own Limitations

INTJ: Understand and Break Free From Your Own Limitations

ENTP: Understand and Break Free From Your Own Limitations

ENTJ: Understand and Break Free From Your Own Limitations

successful path towards self-discovery and future success in all areas of your life.

Note from the author

Thank you for purchasing and reading this book. If you enjoyed it or found it useful then I'd really appreciate it if you would post a short review on Amazon. I do read all the reviews personally so that I can continually write what people are wanting.

If you'd like to leave a review then please visit the link below:

https://www.amazon.com/dp/B07BNKWNWV

Thanks for your support and good luck!

Check Out My Other Books

Below you'll find some of my other books that are popular on Amazon and Kindle as well. Simply search the titles listed below on Amazon. Alternatively, you can visit my author page on Amazon to see other work written by me.

ENFP: Understand and Break Free From Your Own Limitations

INFP: Understand and Break Free From Your Own Limitations

ENFJ: Understand and Break Free From Your Own Limitations

INFJ: Understand and Break Free From Your Own Limitations

ENFP: INFP: ENFJ: INFJ: Understand and Break Free From Your Own Limitations – The Diplomat Bundle Series

INTP: Understand and Break Free From Your Own Limitations

INTJ: Understand and Break Free From Your Own Limitations

ENTP: Understand and Break Free From Your Own Limitations

ENTJ: Understand and Break Free From Your Own Limitations

ESTJ: Understand and Break Free From Your Own Limitations

ISTJ: Understand and Break Free From Your Own Limitations

ISFJ: Understand and Break Free From Your Own Limitations

ESFJ: Understand and Break Free From Your Own Limitations

ISFP: Understand and Break Free From Your Own Limitations

ESTP: Understand and Break Free From Your Own Limitations

ISTP: Understand and Break Free From Your Own Limitations

OPTION B: F**K IT - How to Finally Take Control Of Your Life And Break Free From All Expectations. Live A Limitless, Fearless, Purpose Driven Life With Ultimate Freedom

Printed in Germany
by Amazon Distribution
GmbH, Leipzig